A Note to Parents

DK READERS is a compelling new program for beginning readers, designed in conjunction with leading literacy experts, including Dr. Linda Gambrell, Director of the School of Education at Clemson University. Dr. Gambrell has served on the Board of Directors of the International Reading Association and as President of the National Reading Conference.

Beautiful illustrations and superb full-color photographs combine with engaging, easy-to-read stories to offer a fresh approach to each subject in the series. Each DK READER is guaranteed to capture a child's interest while developing his or her reading skills, general knowledge, and love of reading.

The five levels of DK READERS are aimed at different reading abilities, enabling you to choose the books that are exactly right for your child:

Pre-level 1: Learning to read
Level 1: Beginning to read
Level 2: Beginning to read alone
Level 3: Reading alone
Level 4: Proficient readers

The "normal" age at which a child begins to read can be anywhere from three to eight years old, so these levels are intended only as a general guideline.

No matter which level you select, you can be sure that you are helping your child learn to read, then read to learn!

A DK PUBLISHING BOOK
www.dk.com

Editor Dawn Sirett
Art Editor Jane Horne

Senior Editor Linda Esposito
Senior Art Editor Diane Thistlethwaite
US Editor Regina Kahney
Production Melanie Dowland
Picture Researcher Cynthia Frazer
Jacket Designer Piers Tilbury
Illustrator Gill Tomblin
Specially commissioned photography
Steve Gorton
Building Consultant David Jeffrie

Reading Consultant
Linda B. Gambrell, Ph.D.

First American Edition, 2000
12 13 14 15 14 13
Published in the United States by DK Publishing, Inc.
375 Hudson Street, New York, New York 10014
016-KP840-Mar/2000
Copyright © 2000 Dorling Kindersley Limited, London

Published in Great Britain by Dorling Kindersley Limited.

Eyewitness Readers™ is a trademark of Dorling Kindersley Limited, London.

Library of Congress Cataloging-in-Publication Data

Wallace, Karen.
Big machines / by Karen Wallace.
p. cm. -- (Eyewitness readers)
Summary: Demonstrates how the crane, bulldozer, dump truck, and
other construction machines all play a part in building a new park.
ISBN-13: 978-0-7894-5412-6 (hbk.) -- ISBN-13: 978-0-7894-5411-9 (pbk.)

1. Construction equipment--Juvenile literature. [1. Construction
equipment. 2. Machinery.] I. Title. II. Series.

TH900.W34 2000
624.21--dc21   99-043607

Color reproduction by Colourscan, Singapore
Printed and bound in China by L Rex Printing Co., Ltd.

The publisher would like to thank the following for
their kind permission to reproduce their photographs:
Key: a=above, c=center, b=below, l=left, r=right, t=top
Mark Azavedo Photolibrary: 26; **Sylvia Cordaiy Photo Library Ltd**:
Humphrey Evans 20–21, 20 t; **Ecoscene**: Ian Harwood 6–7; **Pictor
International**: front cover background t, 4–5, 31 t; **Powerstock
Photolibrary/Zefa**: 12–13, 14–15; **Quadrant Picture Library**: 10–11,
16–17; **Telegraph Colour Library**: Gloria H. Chomica front cover
background b, Mark Mattock/Planet Earth 8–9; **Travel Ink**:
Leslie Garland 18–19, Tony Page 18 inset, 32 crb.
Additional credits: Jenifer Hourle, Peter Kindersley Junior, and Wilfrid
Wood (for appearing in this book); Hampstead Garden Centre, London (for
forklift truck and plants); Paul Bricknell, Mike Dunning, and Richard Leeney
(additional photography for DK); Andrea Sadler (additional picture research).

 **READERS**

BEGINNING
1
TO READ

Big Machines

Written by Karen Wallace

DK Publishing, Inc.

BIG machines do BIG jobs.
They can knock down
an old factory.

They can build a new park.
But how do big machines work?

A crane has a heavy ball.
The ball swings through the air.
CRASH!

It smashes into the factory wall!
Bricks and rubble
fall to the ground.

rubble

SMASH!

CRASH!

SMASH!

7

A bulldozer has a huge blade.

SCRAPE!

SCRUNCH!

SCRAPE!

It pushes the rubble into a pile.

What will take

the pile of rubble away?

blade

A loader scoops up the rubble with a huge metal bucket.

The bucket dumps the rubble into a truck.

The truck takes the rubble away.

But where
is the truck?

bucket

Here comes the dump truck!
The dump truck has wide wheels
that can roll over bumpy ground.
It has high sides
so the rubble doesn't fall out.

wheel

The factory has gone.
It is time to build a pond
for the park.
An excavator (EX-kuh-vay-ter)
digs a hole.
An excavator has a bucket
with metal teeth
that break up
the earth.

The bucket
dumps the earth
into a tipper truck.

But where
is that truck?

teeth/

Here comes the tipper truck!
It is carrying new soil
for the park.

The back of the truck
goes up
and the tailgate opens.
WHOOSH! WHOOSH!

The soil slides
onto the ground.

WHOOSH!
WHOOSH!

tailgate

The pond needs concrete
to line its base.
A concrete mixer
brings concrete.
Its drum goes
around and around
and concrete pours out
of a special chute.

chute

When the concrete sets
it is hard and waterproof.

The pond is finished,
but now it needs water.
Here comes a water truck!

It has a big tank full of water
to fill up the pond.

The park needs a path
for people to walk on.

A roller has water
inside its wheels
to make the wheels heavy.

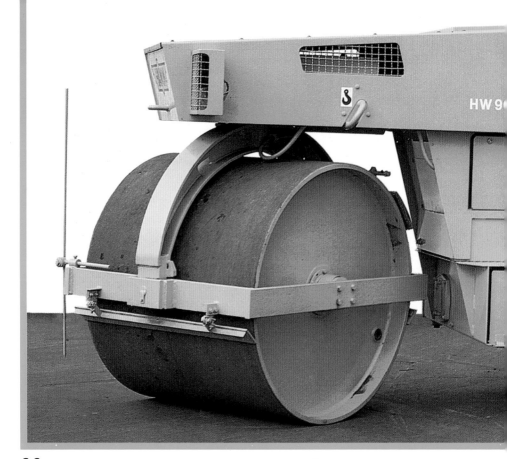

They press down on the path
until it is smooth and flat.

The park needs grass
for children to play on.
A forklift truck brings new turf.
Long forks lift up the turf
and carry it across
the park.

forks

The park needs plants.
A van brings trees and flowers.

Insects, animals, and birds
will make the park their home.

The park needs a playground.
A big truck brings
swings and slides!
Big trucks carry things
all over the world.

Now the park is finished.

Children play on the grass.
People walk on the path.
Birds sing in the trees.
Can you remember
when the factory was there?

This man does.

BIG changes have happened
thanks to BIG machines
that can do BIG jobs!

Picture Word List

rubble

page 6

teeth/

page 15

blade

page 8

tailgate

page 17

bucket

page 11

chute

page 18

wheel

page 13

forks

page 25